FABULOUS FROGS

BY LINDA GLASER
PICTURES BY LORETTA KRUPINSKI

THE MILLBROOK PRESS   BROOKFIELD, CONNECTICUT

Outside by the pond, I hear the frogs sing.

They all call at once in the evenings in spring.

Crick crick. Gribber crick.
Peep peep. Peep peep.

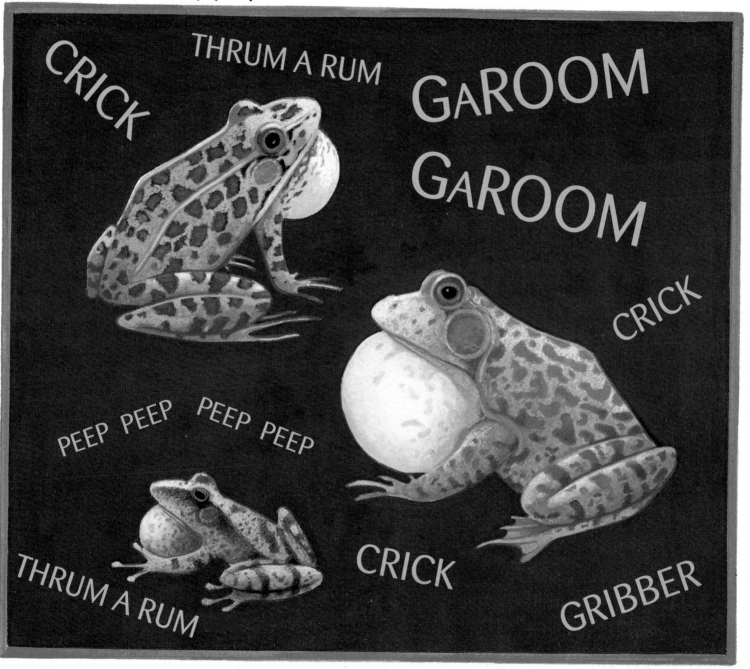

Thrum a rum. Thrum a rum.
GaROOM. GaROOM.

Each kind of frog has its own call to sing.

Father frogs call mother frogs,
who come to the water to listen.

The two swim together.
And together they form
soft living eggs called frog spawn.

Inside the eggs, the soft
dark centers grow. Soon
they turn into tiny tadpoles.

They wiggle in the water,
and eat, and grow,

and change. . .

and change. . .

and change. . .

. . . until they're frogs!

Now they live on land and water.

In puddles and ponds and lakes
and streams they kick and glide
and swim and hide.

On land they hide where they blend in. . .

. . . because lots of hungry animals hunt for them.

A frog has long back legs,
strong back legs

And when it jumps, it

J U M P S

And when it leaps, it

L E A P S

And when it sits, it sits stone still.

It has two big eyes on top of its head to see all around without moving or making a sound.

A hungry frog sits and watches until. . .

a fly lands nearby

ZIP. . .

Frog shoots out its tongue

FLICK. . .

Frog catches that fly and gulps it down

QUICK.

Frog sits very quietly catching
bug after bug just flicking its
quicker-than-quick sticky tongue.

Frogs are my fabulous bug-catching friends.
They are super swimmers

and jumpers

and singers.

Each year they bring their call of spring.

Crick, crick. Gribber crick.
Peep peep. Peep peep.
Thrum a rum. Thrum a rum.
GaROOM. GaROOM.

FABULOUS FACTS ABOUT FROGS

For children who are curious to know more about frogs, here are some answers to questions they may have.

LEOPARD FROG

SPRING PEEPER

BULL-FROG

WHAT TYPES OF FROGS ARE IN THIS BOOK?
Leopard frogs, spring peepers, bullfrogs.

WHAT'S THE DIFFERENCE BETWEEN FROGS AND TOADS?
Frogs and toads look very much alike. Here are some ways to tell most frogs and most toads apart.

WHY ARE FROGS SLIPPERY?
Frogs need to be wet and cool in order to stay alive. Their wet skin helps them breathe. Frogs also absorb water through their wet skin, instead of drinking water with their mouths. Plus slippery skin helps frogs slip away from animals that try to catch them.

TOAD

MOST FROGS	MOST TOADS
have smooth damp skin	have dry bumpy skin
have long back legs	have short back legs
can take long leaps	can take short hops
can be found in water	can be found in woods
live near water	live farther from water
have narrow bodies	have plump bodies

HOW FAR CAN A FROG LEAP?

Most frogs can leap ten lengths of their body in one leap. Try this: Measure your height. Now measure ten times your height on the ground. If you were a frog, you could jump that far in one leap!

HOW LONG DO FROGS LIVE?

The frogs in this book usually live between two and six years. Some kinds of frogs can live from ten to twenty years or more.

WHAT ARE THOSE BIG BULGES ON A FROG'S FACE?

They are air sacs. A frog has two air sacs on either side of its mouth or one air sac under its chin. When a male frog sings, it pulls air into the air sac. The air sac puffs up like a balloon. This makes the frog's song sound much louder.

WHERE ON EARTH DO FROGS LIVE?

Frogs live almost everywhere on Earth except the arctic regions. Some kinds of frogs even live in deserts. Some desert frogs sleep underground for ten years until the rains come!

WHERE DO FROGS GO IN WINTER?

In cold climates, frogs burrow in holes or in the muddy bottoms of ponds and lakes in winter. They hibernate there until spring.

HOW LONG HAVE FROGS LIVED ON EARTH?

Scientists believe that frogs have lived on Earth for 230 millions years. Frogs were here even before dinosaurs.

HOW MANY TYPES OF FROGS ARE THERE?

There are probably about 4,100 types of frogs living on Earth. Here are a few frogs and the fabulous things they do:

- ✦ *The Flying Frog of Borneo* steers in the air with webbed hands and feet.
- ✦ *The Leopard Frog of North America* can jump more than 5 feet (1½ meters).
- ✦ *The Mexican Spoon-headed Frog* backs into a hole and fits in tight as a cork so its enemies can't get it out.
- ✦ *The male Hip Pocket Frog* carries tadpoles in pouches on either side of its body.
- ✦ *The Glass Frog* has see-through skin.
- ✦ *The Smoky Jungle Frog* makes a "nest" for her eggs. She beats the jelly around the eggs into a froth, and the tadpoles grow in this.
- ✦ *The male Darwin Frog* swallows the eggs the female lays. After two months, he opens his mouth and little baby frogs hop out!
- ✦ *The Australian Water-holding Frog* lives in the desert and stores water in its body. Aborigine people squeeze this frog to get water.
- ✦ *The Spring Peeper* sings a high clear call that can be heard a mile away.
- ✦ *The Dwarf Puddle Frog* is the size of a peanut and can eat one hundred mosquitoes in one night!
- ✦ *The African Bull Frog* is as big as a football.
- ✦ *The Paradoxical Frog* of Trinidad shrinks as it grows up. Tadpoles are over 1 foot (30 centimeters) long. But full-grown frogs are only 1½ inches (4 centimeters) long!

WHICH INSECTS DO FROGS EAT?

Frogs eat many kinds of insects, including mosquitoes, flies, dragonflies, and many insect "pests" that eat plants and food crops. Frogs also eat snails, slugs, centipedes, and earthworms.

WHICH ANIMALS EAT FROGS?

Many animals on land, air, and water depend on frogs, tadpoles, or frog eggs for food.

SOME ANIMALS THAT EAT FROGS

Foxes, rats, raccoons, skunks, minks, otters, snakes, turtles, other frogs, large fish, owls, crows, hawks, and waterbirds such as egrets and herons. Some people eat frogs' legs.

SOME ANIMALS THAT EAT TADPOLES

Ducks and other waterbirds, newts, snakes, turtles, large frogs, fish, and water insects.

SOME ANIMALS THAT EAT FROG EGGS

Turtles, fish, and some frogs.

WHY ARE FROGS IMPORTANT TO THE EARTH?

✦ Frogs help keep the insect population under control.

✦ Frogs are an important part of the food chain. This means that many types of animals eat frogs for food. Without frogs, many other animals might not have food to live.

✦ Frogs are unique and amazing animals. They add to the wonder of life on Earth.

ARE FROGS IN ANY DANGER?

Yes. Scientists and environmentalists are concerned because some types of frogs are dying out. And recently, deformed frogs have been discovered.

WHY ARE FROGS IN DANGER?

Frogs are in danger because of problems created by people. Much of the Earth's air and water is no longer clean. Frogs' sensitive skin absorbs both air and water. When the air and water aren't clean, it hurts frogs. Here are some of the problems that frogs face:

✦ Water pollution. Oil spills and other chemicals, plus detergents and trash dumped in the water, kill frogs.

- Pesticides (bug poisons) and herbicides (weed killers) sprayed on fields and lawns kill frogs and kill the insects that frogs eat.

- The thinning of the ozone layer seems to be hurting frogs around the world because more ultraviolet rays from the sun are reaching frogs. Some scientists think that this may be the cause of some frogs dying out and being deformed.

- For unknown reasons, there have recently been deformed frogs found in the United States. Scientists are trying to figure out why this is happening.

- Destruction of frogs' homes or habitats. People fill ponds, lakes, and streams (frogs' homes) with land to build more roads, highways, buildings and houses. When frogs lose their homes, they die.

WHAT CAN PEOPLE DO TO HELP FROGS?

- Protect frogs' homes or habitats. Help save wetlands.

- Build new ponds for frogs to live in.

- Help keep the Earth's air, land, and water clean and free of pesticides, herbicides, and other dangerous chemicals.

- Buy organic foods. Organic food is grown without pesticides, herbicides, and other dangerous chemicals.

- Garden organically without pesticides or herbicides on lawns and gardens.

- Learn about frogs, and share what you've learned with other people.

- Support organizations working to save wetlands and wetland-animal habitats, including frogs' habitats.

Here are a few of the many worthwhile organizations working to save wetlands:

The Nature Conservancy
1815 North Lynn Street
Arlington, Virginia 22209

Rainforest Action Network
221 Pine Street
Suite 500
San Francisco, CA 94104

Clean Water Action
4455 Connecticut Ave. NW
Suite A 300
Washington, D.C. 20008-2328

To my fabulous writers' group:
Katharine Johnson, Margi Preus, Ann Treacy,
Maryann Weidt

Special thanks to William Holmstrom from
the Wildlife Conservation Society and to
Deb Panietz Carroll, a fabulous frog consultant.
LG

Library of Congress Cataloging-in-Publication Data
Glaser, Linda.
Fabulous frogs / by Linda Glaser: pictures by Loretta Krupinski.
p.   cm
Summary: Simple text and illustrations present the physical characteristics,
habits, and life cycle of the frog. Includes a separate question-and-answer
section with more information about the different kinds, their way of life,
and endangered status.
ISBN 0-7613-0424-X (lib. bdg.)
1. Frogs—Juvenile literature. [1. Frogs. 2. Frogs—Miscellanea. 3. Questions
and answers.] I. Krupinski, Loretta, ill. II. Title.
QL668.E2G57   1999
597.8'9—dc21   98-8323   CIP   AC

Published by The Millbrook Press, Inc.
2 Old New Milford Road
Brookfield, Connecticut 06804